EPITAPHS FOR
THE POETS

February 6, 1564 – May 30, 1593

Kit Marlowe had a golden tongue
Which was cut short when he was stabbed
In his right eye, not in the lung.

Epitaphs for the Poets

Editor: Clarinda Harriss
Graphic design: Ace Kieffer

BrickHouse Books, Inc. 2012
306 Suffolk Road
Baltimore, MD 21218

Distributor: Itasca Books, Inc.

ISBN: 978-1-938144-01-1

Printed in the United States of America

OTHER BOOKS BY WESLI COURT

The Gathering of the Elders and Other Poems, 2010

The Collected Lyrics of Lewis Turco / Wesli Court, 1953-2004, 2004

The Airs of Wales, 1981

Curses and Laments, 1978

Murgatroyd and Mabel, 1978

Courses in Lambents, Poems 1977

DEDICATION

Remembering the lives in poetry of my dear old friends, the late

Loring Williams and Charlie Davis.

Acknowledgments

The modern version of William Dunbar's "Lament for the Poets" was first published in Wesli Court's *Courses in Lambents*, Oswego: Mathom Publishing Co., 1977; it and three or four of the epitaphs appeared in one edition or another of *The Book of Forms, A Handbook of Poetics*, Lebanon, NH: University Press of New England, © 1986, 2000, and 2012, used here by permission of the author, Lewis Turco.

Most of the epitaphs appeared online serially in Lewis Turco's blog *Poetics and Ruminations* over a period of five years, 2007-2011.

The oldest of these epitaphs, written on members of the Iowa Writers' Workshop of 1959-60, appeared originally in Part Two of Wesli Court's satire on contemporary American poetry titled "Odds Bodkin's Strange Thrusts and Ravels" published in *The Oberlin Quarterly* in 1966, all rights reserved by Lewis Turco. The whole of the satire was reprinted, first, in *Poetry: An Introduction through Writing*, Reston, VA: Reston Publishing Co. © 1973, copyright reversion to Lewis Turco and all rights reserved; second, in *The Collected Lyrics of Lewis Turco / Wesli Court 1953-2004*, Scottsdale, AZ: Star Cloud Press, © Lewis Turco 2004, by permission of the author, Lewis Turco, and the publisher.

Four of the epitaphs appeared originally in *The Hampden-Sydney Poetry Review* in 2007, by permission of the author, Lewis Turco, and the editor.

Thirty-five of the epitaphs were published online as "A Calendar of Epitaphs" in the *Per Contra Spring 2009 Light Verse Supplement*, by permission of the author, Lewis Turco, and the editor.

Thirteen of the epitaphs appeared online in *The Flea* in 2011, by permission of the author and the editor.

The envoy, "For the Unknown Poets," appeared in *Trinacria* in 2012.

"The Mews of Poetry" was published online in *The Tower Journal* in 2011.

Seven of these epitaphs appeared on-line in *Pen and Parchment* in 2012.

Table of Contents

PROLOGUE : WILLIAM DUNBAR'S LAMENT FOR THE POETS

I who was in health and gladness
Am troubled now with great sickness,
Enfeebled with infirmity;
Fear of death disturbeth me.

Our pleasance here is all vainglory,
This false world is but transitory,
The flesh is fragile, the Fiend is sly;
Timor mortis conturbat me.

The state of man does change and vary
Now sound, now sick; now blithe, now sorry,
Now dancing merry, now like to die;
Timor mortis conturbat me.

No state on earth here stands staunch.
As with the wind waves the branch,
So waves this world's vanity;
Timor mortis conturbat me.

Unto Death go all estates,
Princes, prelates, and potentates,
Both rich and poor, of each degree;
Timor mortis conturbat me.

He takes the knight in the field
Armed under helm and shield —
He is victor of the melee;
Timor mortis conturbat me.

That merciless and tyrant king
Takes, on the mother's breast suckling,
The babe full of benignity;
Timor mortis conturbat me.

He takes the champion of power,
The captain sheltered in his tower,
The embowered lady in her beauty;
Timor mortis conturbat me.

He spares no lord for his puissance,
Nor clerk for his intelligence;
His awful stroke may no man flee;
Timor mortis conturbat me.

Neither astrologers nor magicians,
Clerics, scholars, or logicians
Find help in their conclusions sly;
Timor mortis conturbat me.

Those most learned in medicines —
Leeches, surgeons, and physicians —
May not cure their mortality;
Timor mortis conturbat me.

I see that poets sing their sheaf,
Play their pageant, then go to grief;
Death does not spare their faculty;
Timor mortis conturbat me.

He had to impetuously devour
The noble Chaucer, the poets' flower;
Will of the Plow, and Gower, all three;
Timor mortis conturbat me.

The Bard of "The Pearl" he has slain,
Who wrote "The Adventures of Gawain"
Sir Gilbert Hay — ended has he;
Timor mortis conturbat me.

The good Sir Hugh of Eglinton
And also Heriot and Winton
He has torn from this country;
Timor mortis conturbat me.

Holland and Barbour he has bereft;
Alas! that he could not have left
Sir Mungo Lockert of the Lee;
Timor mortis conturbat me.

That evil scorpion has brought to wreck
Master John Clarke and James Affleck
From ballad-making and tragedy;
Timor mortis conturbat me.

He has Blind Harry and Sandy Traill
Slain with his shower of mortal hail,
Which Patrick Johnston could not flee;
Timor mortis conturbat me.

He's taken Ralph of Aberdeen
And gentle Ralph of Corstophin —
Two better fellows may no man see;
Timor mortis conturbat me.

Now in Dumferlintown he's done
With Master Robert Henryson;
Sir John of Ross has bent his knee;
Timor mortis conturbat me.

And he has taken in his maw
Good, gentle Strobo and Quentin Shaw
On whom all creatures have pity;
Timor mortis conturbat me.

Good Master Walter Kennedy
In point of deed lies verily —
It were great ruth that such should be;
Timor mortis conturbat me.

Since all my brothers thus are gone,
He will not let me live alone;
I may perforce his next prey be;
Timor mortis conturbat me.

Since for the dead there is no cure,
We'd best prepare for what is sure
That we may live eternally;
Timor mortis conturbat me.

R.I.P. JOHN GOWER
c. 1330 – October 1408

Dunbar wept for the Monk of Bery
And John Gower who lived at Overy
Where he was buried in a tomb
That was larger than any womb.

R.I.P. GEOFFREY CHAUCER
c. 1342 – October 25, 1400

The first great poet of our tongue,
He died while relatively young.
They buried him in Westminster,
But no one's sure exactly where.

R.I.P. ROBERT HENRYSON
c. 1425 – 1500

Dunbar sang in his "Lament"
Of Traill, Blind Harry and Tranent,
But most of all in Dumferlintown
He rued good Robert Henryson.

R.I.P. WILLIAM DUNBAR
c. 1460 – 1500

His fellow poets all were taken,
A fact that was beyond his ken,
But he'd not likely be forsaken —
Dunbar was right: he cannot waken.

R.I.P. JOHN SKELTON

c. 1460 – June 21, 1529

Here lies John Skelton
Worn to a skeleton
By tumbling in verse,
For he loved to curse
Or, even worse,
Fulminate, excoriate,
And dub himself "Laureate."

R.I.P. SIR THOMAS WYATT

1503 – October 11, 1542

He fell in love with Anne Boleyn
Yet somehow saved his precious skin
And introduced the English sonnet
Which Shakespeare stole from Thomas Wyatt.

R.I.P. HENRY HOWARD

1517 – January 19, 1547

He and his friend Sir Thomas Wyatt
Were fathers of the English sonnet
Which did no good, for the puppet jury
Condemned to death the Earl of Surrey.

R.I.P. GEORGE PUTTENHAM

c. 1529 – 1590

His *Arte of English Poesy*
Made him a scholar known to be
A womanizing, rutting ram,
Our ancient Cousin Puttenham.

R.I.P. SIR WALTER RALEIGH
c. January 22, 1552 – Oct 29, 1618

A seeker after wealth and power,
He spent some time in London's Tower
After he unwisely wed —
And then Sir Walter lost his head.

R.I.P. EDMUND SPENSER
c. 1552 – January 13, 1599

His vast romance, "The Faerie Queene,"
Cannot be read but may be seen
To need the work of a condenser —
Too late, we fear, for Edmund Spenser.

R.I.P. SIR PHILIP SIDNEY
November 30, 1554 – October 17, 1586

Philip Sidney
Loved his kidney
Pie and sonnets
On shepherdesses
With their tresses
Clad in bonnets.

It's bad enough to have to worry
About Phil Sidney and Howard Surrey,[1]
But I'll be damned, I will be bound,
If I'll lose sleep over Tom[2] and Pound.[3]

---

[1]Henry Howard, Earl of Surrey, 1517 – 19 January 1547; [2] T. S. Eliot, September 26, 1888 – January 4, 1965; [3]Ezra Pound, October 30, 1885 – November 1, 1972.

R.I.P. WILLIAM SHAKESPEARE
April 23, 1564 – April 23, 1616

Word-warrior: when he was spent
He went into retirement.
Although he tried to disappear,
We still hear William shake a spear.

R.I.P. THOMAS CAMPION
February 12, 1567 – March 1, 1620

Thomas Campion loved the lute
But not the trumpet...not a toot,
Nor did he care a bit for rime
Though he wrote lute songs all the time.

R.I.P. BEN JONSON
June 11, 1572 – August 6, 1637

Although convicted of manslaughter,
He preferred to evoke man's laughter
In poems using rime, not con-
sonance, O rare Ben Jonson!

R.I.P. JOHN DONNE
June 19, 1572 – March 31, 1631

He took a playwright's child as bride
And wrote defending suicide,
Used Anne, his wife's name, as a pun
To indicate he was un-Donne,
But he lived longer than did she,
And lingers still in poesy.

R.I.P. MARY WROTH
1587 – 1653

Raleigh, Sidney, Pembroke were her blood;
The Fates therefore took her at their flood
To be a distaff poet cut from cloth
Of gold which made the Muses' Mary Wroth.

R.I.P. ROBERT HERRICK
August 24, 1591 – October 15, 1674

At first a member of the Sons of Ben,
He threw his sermon at a snorer when
Put out to pasture as a country cleric.
The gentry loved their vicar Robert Herrick.

R.I.P. GEORGE HERBERT
April 3, 1593 – March 1, 1633

As good a Christian as he was a man,
Of course it was a part of his Lord's plan
To take the sacred verse that George had sung
With all his heart and wring it from his lung.

R.I.P. THOMAS CAREW
February 1595 – March 22, 1640

When he saw that St. Albans was in bed
Beside the queen, he dropped the candle, said,
"So sorry!" to the king who spotted nary
A thing that eve. The queen waxed good to Carew.

R.I.P. EDMUND WALLER
March 3, 1606 – October 21, 1687

He managed to survive by selling out
His co-conspirators. Never devout,
A shifty man whom some would call a crawler
Was the sly survivor Edmund Waller.

R.I.P. JOHN MILTON
December 9, 1608 – November 8, 1674

The first things that he lost were both his eyes,
The second were the keys to *Paradise*,
Which finally were found. Others built on
This poor foundation the *Parodies* of Milton.

R.I.P. JOHN SUCKLING
February 10, 1609 – June 1, 1642

He took a beating and he lost his pride
To his rival for a disputed bride;
As a rimer he was a sort of duckling —
Or so it's rumored of Sir John Suckling.

R.I.P. ANNE BRADSTREET
March 20, 1612 – September 16, 1672

She hadn't meant to be a poet,
None of her friends, though, seemed to know it:
They published her doodles from the Fleet,
Creating the new bard Anne Bradstreet.

R.I.P. RICHARD CRASHAW
c. 1613 – August 25, 1649

His father was a Protestant divine,
But he himself embraced the Roman line
And wrote in exile verse that veered from coleslaw
To the joyous noise of Richard Crashaw.

R.I.P. RICHARD LOVELACE
1618 – 1657

The female sex adored his looks,
Everyone else adored his books,
Nevertheless, despite success,
He died quite cavalierly loveless.

R.I.P. ABRAHAM COWLEY
December 1618 – July 28, 1667

"What shall I do to be for ever known,"
He wrote, "And make the coming age my own?"
During his lifetime he was famous truly,
But afterward he was treated Cowley.

R.I.P. ANDREW MARVELL
March 31, 1621 – August 16, 1678

He had not world enough, nor time,
For coyness, but enough for rime
To spin its web and develop larval
Verse forms to make Andrew Marvell.

R.I.P. HENRY VAUGHAN
April 17, 1622 – April 23, 1695

He gave the credit for his own survival
To a poet who was not his rival:
George Herbert was his master, he the pawn,
The former was no better, though, than Vaughan.

R.I.P. JOHN DRYDEN
August 9, 1631 – May 13, 1700

When once he learned to write in pairs
Of lines he gave himself no airs
And never after tried to widen
The field of vision of John Dryden.

R.I.P. SAMUEL PEPYS
February 23, 1633 – May 26, 1703

The eminent diarist Pepys
Wrote, "I enter my wife as she sleeps.
    While she is awake,
      For modesty's sake,
She won't let me look while she leaps."

R.I.P. EDWARD TAYLOR
1642 – 1729

He believed God's predetermination,
Wrote each poem as a meditation,
Used the Word as the sharp impaler
Of the sackcloth clothing Edward Taylor.

R.I.P. JOHN GAY
June 30, 1685 – December 4, 1732

Although he had financial trouble
And lost his wealth in the South Sea bubble,
He wrote the famous beggar's play
That made a rich man of John Gay.

R.I.P. ALEXANDER POPE
May 21, 1688 – May 30, 1744

De DUMP de DUMP de DUMP de DUMP de DUMP,
Ka BUMP ka BUMP ka BUMP ka BUMP ka BUMP:
One never needs to flail about or grope
To take the measure of Alexander Pope.

R.I.P. JAMES THOMSON
September 11, 1700 – August 27, 1748

He burned his verse without a tear
On New Year's Day of every year
Until at last our Jemmy Thomson
Wrote an ode for every season.

R.I.P. SAMUEL JOHNSON
September 18, 1709 – December 23, 1784

Many an essay, poem, and play
Fell from his quill in his heyday,
But now we must look in a lexicon
For the words of Doctor Johnson.

R.I.P. WILLIAM SHENSTONE

November 18, 1714 – February 11, 1763

When he retired the poet William Shenstone
Had land but little talent and no pension.
He spent his pounds and talents on a garden
Until his arteries began to harden.
Because he had indulged his flowery ardor,
He had no sustenance left in his larder
And little poesy — hardly a kernel —
To leave upon the pages of his journal.

R.I.P. THOMAS GRAY

December 26, 1716 – July 30, 1771

He wrote but little, published less,
Much to his own and the world's distress,
Till it fell upon him to portray
A "Country Churchyard" in tones of Gray.

R.I.P. CHRISTOPHER SMART

April 11, 1722 – May 21, 1771

When he was young he was a hack,
Or something like one. He'd a knack,
But not much more until his heart
Discovered prayer could make him Smart.

R.I.P. WILLIAM COLLINS

December 25, 1721 – June 12, 1759

He traveled unsuccessful roads,
For no one thought much of his odes,
But now beyond this plot of wall-ins
There is much praise for William Collins.

R.I.P. THOMAS WARTON
January 9, 1728 – May 21, 1790

He wrote, rather inaccurately,
A *History of English Poetry*.
It might have been as well to shorten
The longest work of Thomas Warton.

R.I.P. WILLIAM COWPER
November 26, 1731 – April 25, 1800

Although he was himself bi-polar,
His songs and hymns were popular.
The melancholy William Cowper
Sang on through ecstasy and stupor
And kept on growing just like Topsy
Until at last he died of dropsy.

R.I.P. PHILIP FRENEAU
January 2, 1752 – December 18, 1832

Born between the Classic Age
And the new Romantic rage,
How should he write? He didn't know.
The styles confused Philip Freneau.

R.I.P. THOMAS CHATTERTON
November 20, 1752 – August 24, 1770

Chatterton, the genius boy of Bristol,
Peered through his father's occult ball of crystal,
Invented the ancient poet-priest called Rowley,
Then swallowed poison rather than starve slowly.

R.I.P. WILLIAM BLAKE
November 28, 1757 – August 12, 1827

He saw a "Tyger, burning bright,
In the forests of the night,"
And lived his life, for Heaven's sake,
Until the Night took William Blake.

R.I.P. ROBERT BURNS
January 25, 1759 – July 21, 1796

He wrote a poem "To a Mouse"
And yet another "To a Louse,"
But such were not his great concerns:
His lovers still love Robbie Burns.

R.I.P. MANOAH BODMAN
January 28, 1765 – January 1, 1850

A lawyer who never practiced law,
He spoke with angels that he saw...,
Or were they demons? He was an odd man,
His neighbors thought, old 'Noah Bodman.

R.I.P. S. T. COLERIDGE
October 21, 1772 – July 25, 1834

In Nether Stowey Coleridge
An "Ancient Mariner" decreed
Which there was some need to abridge
Before at last he went to seed.

R.I.P. PHILLIS WHEATLEY
1753 – December 5, 1784

Brought to Boston as the Wheatleys' slave,
She took her freedom to a pauper's grave
With all the learning she had swept up neatly
Into the couplets of Miss Phillis Wheatley.

R.I.P. WILLIAM WORDSWORTH
April 7, 1770 – April 23, 1850

He loved the way the language spills
From one's quill like daffodils
That splash their colors over earth
To give the reader his Wordsworth.

R.I.P. WALTER SCOTT
August 15, 1771 – September 21, 1832

In verse he wrote the Minstrel's Lay
Which made him famous, though not much hay,
But then he discovered how to plot
In prose and died *Sir* Walter Scott.

R.I.P. LEIGH HUNT
October 19, 1784 – August 28, 1859

His lifelong strife with penury
Lasted half a century
But nothing that he tried could blunt
The scythe of the stalker of Leigh Hunt.

R.I.P. PERCY BYSSHE SHELLEY
August 4, 1792 – July 8, 1822

He said to the skylark, "bird thou never wert,"
A line for which no poet would give his shirt,
Nor even a pair of socks that were worn and smelly.
Nevertheless, we honor Percy Shelley.

R.I.P. JOHN CLARE
July 13, 1793 – May 20, 1864

The poorest poet of his age
Or any other, he took his page
From a birch, and from despair
Stole the madness of John Clare.

R.I.P. WILLIAM CULLEN BRYANT
November 3, 1794 – June 12, 1878

When he was seventeen he wrote
The greatest of his poems of note.
"Thanatopsis" was a giant,
But not so William Cullen Bryant.

R.I.P. JOHN KEATS
October 31, 1795 – February 23, 1821

"Here lies one whose name was writ in water"
Is all he asked to be scribed upon his marker,
Yet his best friends — friends but not aesthetes —
Ascribed his death-wish to critics, not John Keats.

R.I.P. GEORGE GORDON, LORD BYRON
January 22, 1788 – April 19, 1824

He never used his club foot on a maiden,
And yet he often managed to get laid in
A damsel's bed. Did cuckolds sometimes fire on
Him if they happened on the poet snorting
Over their panting women? How unsporting
To force the hasty dismount of Lord Byron!

R.I.P. THOMAS HOOD
May 23, 1799 – May 3, 1845

He loved a joke, in particular the pun,
For he was born in London's "Poultry" where,
Perhaps, he first had lots of childhood fun,
And he was introduced to poetry there.

R.I.P. RALPH WALDO EMERSON
May 25, 1803 – April 27, 1882

Here lies Waldo Emerson
Who wished to write for everyone
But not in verse, for Heaven knows
That one can say so much in prose.

R.I.P. ELIZABETH BARRETT BROWNING
March 6, 1806 – June 29, 1861

Her father, Mr. Edward Barrett,
Was certainly a martinet,
But she escaped his constant frowning
When she enjoyed a bit of Browning.

R.I.P. HENRY WADSWORTH LONGFELLOW
February 27, 1807 – March 24, 1882

The first fine bard to come from Maine,
His tongue was lyric, like his brain;
Thus, he wrote verses short and mellow,
But Henry could be a longer fellow.

R.I.P. JOHN GREENLEAF WHITTIER
December 17, 1807 – September 7, 1892

As Abolitionist and Quaker
He was a mover and a shaker,
But as a poet Greenleaf Whittier
Was adequate but hardly wittier.

R.I.P. EDGAR ALLAN POE
January 19, 1809 – October 7, 1849

The darkest poet of his time,
He threw a shadow over rime
And now, beneath this dome of woe,
Erato sleeps with Edgar Poe.

R.I.P. ALFRED TENNYSON
August 6, 1809 – October 6, 1892

The purest poet of his time,
He did nothing else but rime,
So Fate bestowed the benison
Of fame and wealth on Tennyson.

R.I.P. OLIVER WENDELL HOLMES, SR.
August 29, 1809 – October 7, 1894

He never wrote in prose of purple,
Nor were his verses ever puerperal,
And many people loved the pomes
Of Doctor Oliver Wendell Holmes.

R.I.P. ROBERT BROWNING
May 7, 1812 – December 12, 1889

Robert Browning fled his garret
To elope with old maid Barrett.
At last she died and he became
Himself a poet with a name.

R.I.P. EDWARD LEAR
May 12, 1812 – January 29, 1888

Here lies the ridiculous Lear
Whose verses were never too clear,
    For he'd make up a word
    That was rather absurd
And enfabulate it with a leer.

R.I.P. JONES VERY
August 28, 1813 – May 8, 1880

God used to whisper in his ear,
Deliver sonnets loud and clear
But mostly dull and never merry
To the Quietist Jones Very.

R.I.P. JOHN GODFREY SAXE
June 2, 1816 – March 31, 1887

Laws are much like sausages —
The more we know of how they're made,
The more we are their hostages,
He wrote, and feel they're retrograde.

R.I.P. ARTHUR HUGH CLOUGH
January 1, 1819 – November 13, 1861

He didn't like religion much —
All that ritual and such,
So Oxford was a little rough
On the poet Arthur Clough.

R.I.P. JAMES RUSSELL LOWELL
February 22, 1819 – August 12, 1891

He loved to warm himself beside
His fellows of the Fireside
Where he could roast them in the fire
Upon the spit of his satire.

R.I.P. WALT WHITMAN
May 31, 1819 – March 26, 1892

He wooed his Muse but couldn't metre,
And so he thought he'd try to cheat her
By stifling her till she was smitten
By the prose of Walter Whitman.

R.I.P. MATTHEW ARNOLD
December 24, 1822 – April 15, 1888

He was arthritic as a critic,
Only slightly worser as a verser,
Something of a Trojan as a theologian —
Earth broke the mold of Matthew Arnold.

R.I.P. DANTE GABRIEL ROSSETTI
May 12, 1828 – April 9, 1892

Higgledy-piggledy
Dante Rossetti
Tried to revive the
Darkest of ages

With the Pre-Raphaelites
Moving Aesthetically
Out of the Gothic and
Into new rages.

R.I.P. CHRISTINA ROSSETTI
December 5, 1830 – December 29, 1894

Higgledy-piggledy
Christina Rossetti be-
Came with her family
Anglified Protestants

Just like her brothers Pre-
Raphaelitically
Eschewing society's
Talentless debutantes.

R.I.P. EMILY DICKINSON
December 10, 1830 – May 15, 1886

The Maid of Amherst, Emily
Dickinson, sang quietly
Far from the roar of the madding throng,
But now she holds her breath too long.

R.I.P. LEWIS CARROLL
January 27, 1832 – January 14, 1898

And glying came the Wamble Dog
Barking Lewis Carroll,
He met up with the Bandersnatch,
And threw him in a barrel.

R.I.P. BRET HARTE
August 25, 1836 – May 6, 1902

He rode and wrote about the booming West,
Its roaring camps – he seemed to be obsessed
With it, but when he found he could depart,
The West found it had lost its own Bret Harte.

R.I.P. ALGERNON CHARLES SWINBURNE,

INVENTOR OF THE ROUNDEL VERSE FORM;
April 5, 1837 – April 10, 1909

Was he gay, or merely callow
As Oscar Wilde would often say?
It was too much for Wilde to swallow.
   Was he gay?

More prone to brag than likely stray,
His reputation was too hollow
For Oscar whom he could not sway.

His standing has been lying fallow
For a century today
And likely for the years that follow.
   Was he gay?

R.I.P. AUSTIN DOBSON

January 18, 1840 – September 2, 1921

Austin Dobson wrote in verse
Forms he found in France. Perverse?
Indeed. He did it anyway,
But he has little more to say.

R.I.P. THOMAS HARDY

June 2, 1840 – January 11, 1928

He always wished to be a poet
And ever wished that he could show it
To the world, but the word was tardy
For the novelist Thomas Hardy.

R.I.P. SIDNEY LANIER
February 3, 1842 – September 7, 1881

The southerner Sidney Lanier
Lies in his coffin coughing here
No longer; he wants no resumption
Of his Civil War consumption.

R.I.P. ROBERT BRIDGES
October 23, 1844 – April 21, 1930

He thought that poets ought to reach
For levels of ordinary speech,
Not overflow the averages
That run beneath the span of Bridges.

R.I.P. EUGENE FIELD
September 2, 1850 – November 4, 1895

"Wynken, Blynken, and Nod one night
Sailed off in a wooden shoe,
Sailed on a river of crystal light
Into a sea of dew,"
And then, upon another night
'Gene Field did that too.

R.I.P. ELLA WHEELER WILCOX
November 5, 1850 – October 30, 1919

Her husband said that when he died
He'd come and visit, but he lied.
Emma in her baffled grief
Felt he'd betrayed their shared belief
And she could never understand
Why he hid his head beneath the sand.

R.I.P. EDWIN MARKHAM
April 23, 1852 – March 7, 1940

"Man with a Hoe," his greatest lay,
Means something different today.

R.I.P. A. E. HOUSMAN
March 26, 1859 – April 30, 1936

He wasn't good, he wasn't bad,
He was simply always sad,
This Shropshire lad who wore a caftan
Woven of shadow, Alfred Housman.

R.I.P. HAMLIN GARLAND
September 14, 1860 – March 4, 1940

He wrote plain stuff about the far land
Of the West, but Hamlin Garland
Preferred to live in New England,
For he preferred his foodstuffs canned.

R.I.P. WILLIAM BUTLER YEATS
June 13, 1865 – January 28, 1939

He wrote that "Love has pitched his tent
In the place of excrement."
Alas! That's how this world creates
The likes of William Butler Yeats.

R.I.P. RUDYARD KIPLING
December 30, 1865 – January 18, 1936

He left Vermont because his tippling
Brother-in-law threatened Kipling.
In Britain he found that his guerdon
Was shouldering the White Man's Burden.

R.I.P. GELETT BURGESS

January 30, 1866 – September 18, 1951

He never saw a purple cow,
He never hoped to see one,
But I can tell you anyhow,
Gelett thought they were gorgeous.

R.I.P. EDGAR LEE MASTERS

August 23, 1868 – March 5, 1950

When he was young he learned to spoon
Beneath the white Midwestern moon.
He had success and then disasters:
Spoon River drowned Edgar Masters.

R.I.P. EDWIN ARLINGTON ROBINSON

December 22, 1869 – April 6, 1935

He lived in Gardiner, Maine, called it his own,
Though he renamed the place "Tilbury Town"
And hated it. It was the skeleton
Which he fleshed with the *Corpus Robinson*.

R.I.P. HILAIRE BELLOC

July 27, 1870 – July 16, 1953

He hoped when he was dead it might be said,
"His sins were scarlet but his books were read."
But one must sigh and cry, "Alas! Alack!
Hilaire has largely lost his Belloc clacque!"

R.I.P. JAMES WELDON JOHNSON
June 17, 1871 – June 26, 1938

He wrote a book called *God's Trombones* —
According to James Nathan Jones
He heard them in Wiscasset, Maine,
When he died mangled by a train.

R.I.P. RALPH HODGSON
September 9, 1871 – November 3, 1962

He wrote a modern Mother Goose
Sort of poem, very loose
Of metre, with a heavy beat
That even Death cannot defeat.

R.I.P. PAUL LAURENCE DUNBAR
June 27, 1872 – February 9, 1906

A wunderkind chock-full of gumption,
He died at thirty-three of consumption.

R.I.P. WALTER DE LA MARE
April 25, 1873 – June 22, 1956

"Is there anybody there?"
Was the query that he raised
To a house of phantom Listeners —
He would have been amazed
Had someone answered there...,
Answered Walter de la Mare.

R.I.P. ROBERT SERVICE
January 16, 1874 – September 11, 1958

His vein of verse was a lucky strike:
He made a fortune from the Klondike.
Though civilization made him nervous,
France saw most of Robert Service.

R.I.P. GERTRUDE STEIN
February 3, 1874 – July 27, 1946

She wrote, "As everybody knows,
A rose is a rose is a rose is a rose"
And not somebody's Valentine
Nor an anodyne in someone's Stein.

R.I.P. AMY LOWELL
February 9, 1874 – May 12, 1925

She loved cigars and the School of Pound
And soon possessed what she had found;
When it came time for her to pass
She watched her image in the glass.

R.I.P. ROBERT FROST
March 26, l874 – January 29, 1963

Death is, of course, the Thief of Time,
Not to mention an end to rime
Which we discovered to our cost
When we were robbed of Robert Frost.

R.I.P. CARL SANDBURG
January 6, 1878 – July 22, 1967

How Sandburg wrote so much, who knows?
But everything he wrote was prose.

R.I.P. JOHN MASEFIELD
June 1, 1878 – May 12, 1967

He went down to the sea again,
To the lonely sea and the ships,
And that's where Charon was waiting
For Erato to seal his lips.

R.I.P. WALLACE STEVENS
October 2, 1879 – August 2, 1955

"God's a blind that blocks the sun,
Wool pulled over everyone
Who thinks that he can roll elevens
And win death's craps," said Wallace Stevens.

R.I.P. WITTER BYNNER
August 10, 1881 – June 1, 1968

He helped to pull the Spectrist Hoax
With friends — their literary jokes
Were served like Knishes in a diner
By Arthur Ficke and Witter Bynner.

R.I.P. EDGAR GUEST
August 20, 1881 – August 5, 1959

He wrote, "It takes a heap o' livin' to make a house a home,"
And found it took a lot less work to make a rhyming tome,
So rather than become a sort of versifying pest,
He thought he'd move right in and stay an Edgar-present Guest.

R.I.P. JAMES JOYCE

February 2, 1882 – January 13, 1941

He wrote experimental prose
As wild as any could compose,
But avant-gardists could impeach
Joyce's poor *Pomes Penyeach*.

R.I.P. WILLIAM CARLOS WILLIAMS

September 17, 1883 – March 4, 1963

So much depends upon that red
  wheel barrow glazed with rain
    water beside the white chickens,
no doubt – but what? We feel
  someone should tell us but, alas!
    only Doctor Williams could.

R.I.P. PADRAIC COLUM

December 8, 1881 – January 11, 1972

A friend and countryman of Yeats,
He came to the United States
And tried to live by singing solemn
Songs that fell from a Paddy Colum.

R.I.P. ELINOR WYLIE

September 7, 1885 – December 16, 1928

Here lies Elinor Wylie —
Used to the life of Riley,
She wrote about "Wild Peaches"
But not what the wild life teaches.

R.I.P. EZRA POUND
October 30, 1885 – November 1, 1972

He was a young expatriate,
A poet and ex-patriot
Who, like some old disloyal hound,
Was put in the cage of Ezra Pound.

R.I.P. SIEGFRIED SASSOON
September 8, 1886 – September 1, 1967

A hero of the first World War,
He learned to hate, not to adore
Death's instruments and played his tune
Upon Pan's small Sassoon bassoon.

R.I.P. HILDA DOOLITTLE
September 10, 1886 – September 27, 1961

Pound called his friend an "Imagist"
And placed her name upon his list,
But only if she would agree
Initially upon "H. D."

R.I.P. JOYCE KILMER
December 6, 1886 – July 30, 1918

I doubt that I shall ever seize
A poem lousier than "Trees."
Too bad his first name wasn't "Wilmer" —
How much nicer for "Joyce" Kilmer.

R.I.P. ROBINSON JEFFERS
January 10, 1887 – January 20, 1962

He didn't like mankind so well
And thought we all should go to hell.
He loved wild animals, not heifers,
Though they sustained Robinson Jeffers.

R.I.P. EDITH SITWELL
September 7, 1887 – December 9, 1964

She wrote a jazz poem called "Façade,"
As odd as any French ballade
But longer far. It doesn't fit well
With those few who remember Sitwell.

R.I.P. MARIANNE MOORE
November 15, 1887 – February 5, 1972

She loved to rime syllabic verse
In lines that often were not terse,
And she could leave rhopalic spoor
Wherever Marianne might moor.

R.I.P. JOHN CROWE RANSOM
April 30, 1888 – July 3, 1974

A Fugitive from Vanderbilt,
As a southern bard he ran some
Distance then began to wilt —
This critic John Crowe Ransom.

R.I.P. IRVING BERLIN
May 11, 1888 – September 22, 1989

His "Alexander's Ragtime Band"
Were Berlin's first words come to hand,
And when he died at 101
Irving felt he wasn't done.

R.I.P. T. S. ELIOT
September 26, 1888 – January 4, 1965

"The Waste Land" and the "Four Quartets"
Were among his surest bets
For lasting fame, but Eliot's
Good name stands nowadays on "Cats."

R.I.P. CONRAD AIKEN
August 5, 1889 – August 17, 1973

He found his parents' murder-suicide
When he was but a child. Although he tried
His hand at death himself he was not taken
Till age took pity on old Conrad Aiken.

R.I.P. CLAUDE MCKAY
September 15, 1890 – May 22, 1948

Born on the Island of Jamaica,
Claude McKay preferred to make a
Life and livelihood in the pretty
Villages of London and New York City.

R.I.P. E. E. CUMMINGS
October 14, 1890 – September 3, 1962

He wrote no oratorios,
Operas, or vainglorios,
Only the slightly wacky hummings
Of an Edward Estlin Cummings.

R.I.P. COLE PORTER
June 9, 1891 – October 15, 1964

He started writing songs at Yale
But then his Muse began to pale,
Yet he continued as her courter
Until she warmed up to Cole Porter.

R.I.P. EDNA ST. VINCENT MILLAY
February 22, 1892 – October 19, 1950

Edna loved both girls and guys,
A liberal policy if not wise,
For it was difficult to say
Where she might write her latest lay.

R.I.P. ARCHIBALD MACLEISH
May 7, 1892 – April 20, 1982

Here lies Archibald MacLeish.
"A poem should not mean, but be,"
He wrote, for poems should be free
And never kept upon a leash.
He did not do as he was bid,
For that's exactly what he did.

R.I.P. WILFRED OWEN
March 18, 1893 – November 4, 1918

Here lies the poet Wilfred Owen
Who used the powers of his pen
To picture vividly the horror
That swallowed him in the First World War.

R.I.P. DOROTHY PARKER
August 22, 1893 – June 7, 1967

Although she's missed by more than half,
One can but write an epitaph
To note that few dimwits were darker
Than that lightwit Dorothy Parker.

R.I.P. JEAN TOOMER
December 26, 1894 – March 30, 1967

In his background there were numer-
ous genetic lines. Jean Toomer
Was himself a melting pot,
Though he was not a polyglot.

R.I.P. LORENZ HART
May 2, 1895 – November 22, 1943

It is Bewitching to divine
Why one would love a Valentine
As Funny as the counterpart
Of that described by Lorenz Hart.

R.I.P. OSCAR HAMMERSTEIN II
July 12, 1895 – August 23, 1960

When he grew up a golden haze
Began suffusing Broadway's days.
It still won't lift, but we raise wine
To the songs of Oscar Hammerstein.

R.I.P. IRA GERSHWIN
December 6, 1896 – August 17, 1983

His brother did not need to hire a
Lyricist once sibling Ira
Gershwin started writing gorge-
eous words for the tunesmith George
Who died too young, but many a song
They wrote is sung and lingers long.

R.I.P. LOUISE BOGAN
August 11, 1897 – February 4, 1970

Her mother flaunted each affair
Which taught the young Louise to fear
Uncertainty, and thus began
The formal structures of Bogan.

R.I.P. MELVIN B. TOLSON
February 6, 1898 – August 29, 1966

He wrote *The Harlem Group of Negro Writers*
But was himself one of the fearless fighters
Of the heartland, a man of racial mixture,
Part and parcel of his nation's texture.

R.I.P. STEPHEN VINCENT BENET
July 22, 1898 – March 13, 1943

He wrote an epic of the Civil War
That still reverberates from shore to shore,
And *John Brown's Body*'s unlikely to decay
As fast as that of its author, S. V. Benèt.

R.I.P. HART CRANE
July 21, 1899 – April 27, 1932

He took a lot of satisfaction
In big words picturing abstraction,
But he died not of verbiage —
He jumped the rail, not off "The Bridge."

R.I.P. CHARLIE DAVIS
November 18, 1899 – December 12, 1999

He copped a tune that was a pinch of pagan
And named it for a tin of "Copenhagen."
We thank him for the song and dance he gave us
And miss our friend and partner Charlie Davis.

R.I.P. ALLEN TATE
November 19, 1899 – February 9, 1979

He was a Fugitive a while,
And an Agrarian with style,
Who often would Confederate
With poets much like Allen Tate.

R.I.P. LÉONIE ADAMS
December 9, 1899 – June 27, 1988

A poet's poet since she was on a trike,
She never metaverse she didn't like.

R.I.P. LANGSTON HUGHES
February 1, 1902 – May 22, 1967

He found he could write anything,
But he liked best that he could sing
And not be punished for the views
Found in the verse of Langston Hughes.

R.I.P. OGDEN NASH
August 19, 1902 – May 19, 1971

A son of Rye but nephew of the word,
He courted everything that was absurd
And caught it sometimes with élan, panache,
And often with the bite of Ogden Nash.

The poet lives 'twixt prose and verse
Than which no fix can be much worse,
But then along came Ogden Nash
Who turned the whole thing into cash.

R.I.P. COUNTEE CULLEN
May 30, 1903 – January 9, 1946

As soon as he was born he was bereft
Of folks who took one look before they left.
When he got famous his mom shook off her sullen
And got in touch with her honey Countee Cullen.

R.I.P. JOHN HOLMES
January 6, 1904 – June 22, 1962

He thought he made up "Preston Gurney,"
A fictive poet, but on his journey
He swerved and hit a book of poems
Written by Gurney, amazing Holmes.

R.I.P. RICHARD EBERHART
April 5, 1904 – June 9, 2005

He thought the Salem girls were witches
And not in fact demonic bitches
Crying out against the labors
Of the Lord among their neighbors,
So that is what Dick Eberhart
Wrote, for he was ever heart.

R.I.P. PHYLLIS MCGINLEY
March 21, 1905 – February 22, 1978

The comic poet Phyllis McGinley
Climbed Parnassus, not McKinley.

R.I.P. ROBERT PENN WARREN
April 24, 1905 – September 15, 1989

Their *Understanding Poetry*
Was to the academy
The bible he and his partner Brooks
Wrote but at which no one looks.

R.I.P. STANLEY KUNITZ
July 29, 1905 – May 14, 2006

His pseudonym was "Dilly Tante,"
But he read Hegel, Marx and Kant
And lived to be one-hundred-one —
He feels perhaps he may be done.

R.I.P. KENNETH REXROTH
December 22, 1905 – June 6, 1982

His third wife fell in love with Creeley
Because she loved a bit too freely,
But so did he: while still in wedlock
With another, he made her bedrock.

R.I.P. JOHN BETJEMAN
August 28, 1906 – May 19, 1984

He failed, and Oxford's Magdalen sent him down.
But when at last he managed to gain renown
The school discovered they could fetch a man
An honorary "Doctor Betjeman."

R.I.P. W. H. AUDEN
February 21, 1907 – September 29, 1973

When Hitler started raising hell
In Europe, Auden had a smile
For England, said, "A fond farewell —
This British thing is not my style."

R.I.P. A. D. HOPE
July 21, 1907 – July 13, 2000

Here lies, Down Under, A. D. Hope
Who knew the ins-and-outs of trope
And harmonizing prose and metre
To make his lines grander and sweeter.

R.I.P. THEODORE ROETHKE
May 25, 1908 – August 1, 1963

Nurtured in a greenhouse up in Michigan,
A hothouse flower himself, he came to wish again
And yet again that he were a frog or fish again
Whenever he gave himself to poetry,
So swimming took the life of Theodore Roethke.

R.I.P. PAUL ENGLE
October 12, 1908 – March 22, 1991

He was the famous Angler,
Forever politic.
He wheedled sheckels for his boys...,
That always did the trick.

R.I.P. STEPHEN SPENDER
February 28, 1909 – July 16, 1995

A laureate who never spent his time
Trying to pass a test, preferred to rime
And be the gay defender and befriender
Of the dependent masses under Spender.

R.I.P. JOHNNY MERCER
November 18, 1909 – June 25, 1976

He kept his sense of humor, chuckle merry,
Named the Mississippi "Huckleberry";
Of the songsters often he was terser —
There were few as sharp as Johnny Mercer.

R.I.P. FRANK LOESSER
June 29, 1910 – July 29, 1969

Many lyricists were lesser
Men of talents than Frank Loesser.

R.I.P. CHARLES OLSON
December 27, 1910 – January 10, 1970

He read the cant of Ezra Pound
And now he lies beneath this mound
Of rubble, pondering his role, son —
Ezra's avatar, Charles Olson.

R.I.P. ELIZABETH BISHOP
February 8, 1911 – October 6, 1979

She did not wish upon a star,
But wrote about things as they are
Except, of course, when she would dish up
The visions of a roaming Bishop.

R.I.P. J. V. CUNNINGHAM
August 23, 1911 – March 30, 1985

Here he lies in the Winters glade
With hoar-Frost on his shoulderblade:
Now there's no rale in the diaphragm
Of dour, dark J. V. Cunningham.

R.I.P. KENNETH PATCHEN
December 13, 1911 – January 8, 1972

"A waterglass on the bureau fills with morning"
As we consider Kenneth Patchen's verse
Filled with pain but not with that pain's curse.
A ewer on the bureau fills with mourning.

R.I.P. WOODY GUTHRIE
July 14, 1912 – October 3,1967

He wandered all around the place,
He covered lots and lots of space
In what he called "Your land and my land,"
And he could have sung, "*Manhattan* Island."

R.I.P. MAY SWENSON
May 28, 1913– December 4, 1989

May Swenson
Sang the hen song.

R.I.P. WALT KELLY
August 25, 1913 – October 18, 1973

Here lies Pogo's father Walt
Friend and foe of the hale and halt
Who much enjoyed a hammish sangwish
When he wrote in the Anguish languish.

R.I.P. JOHN FREDERICK NIMS
November 20, 1913 – January 13, 1999

Were he alive, he'd pick these lines
To nits, turn wrinkles into wrines.
God now submits his choir's hymns
To *Poetry*'s John Frederick Nims.

R.I.P. ROBERT HAYDEN
August 4, 1913 – February 25, 1980

His "brothahs" thought he was perverse —
An "Uncle Tom" or something worse,
But he felt he need not be laden
With more than simply "Robert Hayden."

R.I.P. KARL SHAPIRO
November 10, 1913 – May 14, 2000

He wrote an ode upon "The Fly"
And hoped his opus would not die,
For if it did there would be zero
Posthumous buzz on Karl Shapiro.

R.I.P. DELMORE SCHWARTZ
December 8, 1913 – July 11, 1966

Beginning with his folks' divorce,
He made their history the force
That drove his life, by all reports,
To the solitude of Delmore Schwartz.

R.I.P. WILLIAM STAFFORD
January 17, 1914 – August 28, 1993

William Stafford couldn't tell
When he had written something well
Although he tried and tried and tried —
His editors had to decide.

R.I.P. WELDON KEES
February 24, 1914 – July 18, 1955

The gods of Fury gave him great success —
Whatever he tried to do those gods would bless.
Therefore, to spite them all he thought he'd seize
Fate at the Golden Gate where Death had Kees.

R.I.P. BARBARA HOWES
May 1, 1914 – February 24, 1996

Beneath this marker made of moss
And this wreath of laurel boughs
Lies the poet Barbara Howes
Who sang of affection and of loss.

R.I.P. RANDALL JARRELL
May 6, 1914 – October 14, 1965

Agrarian and *Fugitive*,
Jarrell could be punitive
When criticizing friends and foes,
Not in his verse but in his prose.

R.I.P. JOHN BERRYMAN
October 25, 1914 – January 7, 1972

His father was a suicide
When John was twelve; therefore, he died
By jumping off a campus span,
Another fated Berryman.

R.I.P. DYLAN THOMAS
October 27, 1914 – November 9, 1953

Some poets don't know how to live;
Their lives seep out as through a sieve,
Leaving behind mostly promise —
Here lies the Welshman Dylan Thomas.

R.I.P. JOHN CIARDI
June 24, 1916 – March 30, 1986

The lately great limerist Ciardi,
Whose muse was nigh onto untardy,
      Whenever he sang
      In his New England twang,
Made rum sounds like, "Paw me a toddy."

R.I.P. JOHN MALCOLM BRINNIN
September 13, 1916 – June 25, 1998

Although he'd shown a lot of promise,
His claim to fame is *Dylan Thomas
In America* where John Brinnin
Washed the Welshman's dirty linen.

R.I.P. ROBERT LOWELL
March 1, 1917 – September 12, 1977

A scion of the House of Lowell
And born with a New England soul,
He wandered far when he left home
And ended in the vaults of Rome.

R.I.P. RADCLIFFE SQUIRES
May 5, 1917 – February 14, 1993

A scholar and an editor
And many a poet's friend and mentor,
Perhaps he now has time for lyres
Proffered by the Muse that Radcliffe Squires.

R.I.P. GWENDOLYN BROOKS
June 7, 1917 – December 3, 2000

When she was young Miss Gwendolyn Brooks
Lost and found herself in books.

R.I.P. LOUIS O. COXE
April 15, 1918 – May 25, 1993

Here lies the poet Louis Coxe
Who once was clever as a fox.
He loved to put to sea and plow
The waves when he remembered how.

R.I.P. ALAN JAY LERNER
August 31, 1918 – June 14, 1986

A stranger sat down at his table
And, fast as they were able,
They fired up their after-burner
Taking off as Loewe and Lerner.

R.I.P. LAWRENCE FERLINGHETTI
March 24, 1919 –

Here lies Lawrence Ferlinghetti
Wrapped in crepes, not in spaghetti
Because he was — by fatal chance —
Not bred in Yonkers but in France.

R.I.P. HOWARD NEMEROV
February 29, 1920 – July 5, 1991

His verse could boil the cosmos down
To the simple stitches of a gown.
But few could be the hemmer of
The skirts of Howard Nemerov.

R.I.P. RICHARD WILBUR
March 1, 1921 –

The finest singer of his time,
He knew the ins-and-outs of rime
Like no one else, but thought the norm
Was that the *poem* chose its form!

R.I.P. MONA VAN DUYN
May 9, 1921 – December 2, 2004

Here lies Mona Jane Van Duyn
Whose poetry was very fine.
She won every prize in sight
Before she slipped into the night.

R.I.P. PHILIP LARKIN
August 9, 1922 – December 2, 1985

He wrote about impending death
In an "Aubade" which is the breath
Of dawn, not night, But dawn would darken
The serenade of Philip Larkin.

R.I.P. JAMES DICKEY
February 2, 1923 – January 19, 1997

He caught his Muse upon the fly
Which made her howl and start to cry.
His evening dress got wet and sticky —
Thus they buried poor James Dickey.

R.I.P. DANIEL HOFFMAN
April 2, 1923 –

In his first book he caught the tails
Of *An Armada of Thirty Whales.*
Since then Dan Hoffman's kept his net
Of words in shape and kept it wet.

R.I.P. DENISE LEVERTOV
October 24, 1923 – December 20, 1997

A pacifist and feminist,
It was one's duty to resist
Violence, yet her pillars
Fell with, "O, to kill the killers!"

R.I.P. RICHARD HUGO
December 21, 1923 – October 22, 1982

Here lies the poet Richard Hugo —
He has gone where very few go
And return, so he is dressed
To lie about and be depressed.

R.I.P. EDWARD FIELD
June 7, 1924 –

If words were straw and prose a cud,
Among these stones we'd hear a thud
From time to time and here, revealed,
We'd find the poems of Edward Field.

R.I.P. JOHN WAIN
March 14, 1925 – May 24, 1994

He joined "The Movement" because he felt
Society deserved the blows they dealt,
But soon enough he felt the pain
Inflicted had begun to Wain.

R.I.P. MAXINE KUMIN
June 6, 1925 –

She wrote as well as she was able,
But when she tired she used the stable
On her farm — that way, of course,
She sometimes grew a little hoarse.

R.I.P. DONALD JUSTICE
August 12, 1925 – August 6, 2004

The lawyer of the Workshop
Enjoyed a rhythmic game.
His first theme was nostalgia —
His last theme was the same.

R.I.P. PHILIP BOOTH
October 8, 1925 – July 2, 2007

He used his brain till it was beaten
And went where brains go when they're eaten,
For Time had used its wisdom tooth
Upon the mind of Philip Booth.

R.I.P. CAROLYN KIZER
December 10, 1925 –

She made the battle of the sexes
Humorous, a fact that vexes
Feminists who are no wiser
For the efforts of Ms. Kizer.

R.I.P. W. D. SNODGRASS
January 5, 1926 – January 13, 2009

There was a professor named Snodgrass,
Who conducted a demigod's class.
His confessional verses
Can be found in the purses
Of many an elderly odd lass.

He never asked his readers' pardons
For sometimes using "S. S. Gardons"
In place of "Snodhrass" — pardon me!
Instead of "h" that should be "g"!

R.I.P. PHILIP APPLEMAN
February 8, 1926 –

"God didn't make little green apples,"
Though it does rain in Indianapolis,
But a maker of dowdy apple-pan
Was Darwin's poet Appleman.

R.I.P. JAMES MERRILL
March 3, 1926 – February 6, 1995

When he was young James Merrill sang
Until the Muses' rafters rang,
But later on he stayed in touch
With phantoms, spirits, ghosts and such.

R.I.P. ROBERT CREELEY
May 21, 1926 – March 30, 2005

He was supposed to be a fountain
Of tough new stuff out of Black Mountain,
But what it came down to was really
A touchy-feely Robert Creeley.

R.I.P. ALLEN GINSBERG
June 3, 1926 – April 5, 1997

Here's Allen, Louis' little son,
Who as a Beat had lots of fun.
His father was a poetaster,
And each of them was a disaster.

R.I.P. DAVID WAGONER
June 5, 1926 –

David Wagoner lies beneath
This Douglas fir wrapped in a wreath
Of poems of the great Northwest.
He wrote them all; they pass the test.

R.I.P. ROBERT BLY
December 23, 1926 –

You need to be a world-wide roamer,
Read Neruda and Tranströmer,
To write verse true as apple pie
Opined the poet Robert Bly,

R.I.P. JOHN ASHBERY
July 28, 1927 –

He spins like a kaleidoscope
From word to word and trope to trope
Until his language honeycomb
Is wholly limned in polychrome.

R.I.P. RICHARD MOORE
September 25, 1927 – November 8, 2009

The poet Richard Moore
Wrote verses that were dour,
Yet others he'd indite
Often could be bright.
Now he has lost his spark
And we are in the dark.

R.I.P. JAMES WRIGHT
December 13, 1927 – March 25, 1980

"Legs up, la la, legs down, la la
Back to sleep again."
James Wright was right to sing that song
When he was young, right now *and* then.

R.I.P. DONALD HALL
September 20, 1928 –

His parents wept, for they both hated
The jobs for which they seemed ill-fated;
He learned to let his teardrops fall
And drown the verse of Donald Hall.

He used to rime, but then he stopped
And turned to sentences he chopped
Up into lines that could merely pall,
And now he wears one: Donald Hall.

R.I.P. ANNE SEXTON
November 9, 1928 – October 4, 1974

Diagnosed a Narcissist
By her psychotherapist,
She studied verse on his advice.
He didn't have to tell her twice —
She had the theme to write her text on:
The mental illness of Anne Sexton.

R.I.P. RICHARD FROST
April 8, 1929 –

He met a poet who shared his name
Once long ago and overcame
His awe, but Fortune never tossed
The palm to the poet *Richard* Frost.

R.I.P. ADRIENNE RICH
May 16, 1929 –

When she was young she caught the itch
To versify and rime, the which
She lost when she began to switch
To the lesbofeministic pitch,
And this became her lifelong niche.

R.I.P. X. J. KENNEDY
August 21, 1929 –

The letter "X" is just an ex,
It's not a blessing or a hex,
Nor will it help you sing a threnody
For the poet X. J. Kennedy.

Here lies, riming while he snoozes,
Joseph Kennedy. May the Muses
If he wakens give him plenty
Of his favorite nepenthe.

R.I.P. THOM GUNN
August 29, 1929 – April 25, 2004

He thought that cooking meth was fun
Until his life was over, done
To a turn: they found Thom Gunn
Had baked a batch of oblivion.

R.I.P. JOHN HOLLANDER
October 28, 1929 –

He never strained for the sublime
Or used a sieve to find a rime,
Yet Time in its broad colander
Has sifted through John Hollander.

R.I.P. GREGORY CORSO
March 26, 1930 – January 17, 2001

He signed the flyleaf of a tome,
"Chow! Chai!" — in every pome
Much of the same, and even moreso
Runs the legacy of Gregory Corso.

R.I.P. MILLER WILLIAMS
April 8, 1930 –

As odd or strange as it may seem to be,
Biology turned into poesy,
But he enjoyed his verses more than plums —
Now here lies our friend Miller Williams.

R.I.P. TED HUGHES
August 17, 1930 – October 28, 1998

*"He often put himself into a trance before he writing,
and he tried to take the point of view of animals."*
— Garrison Keillor.
"

"He often put himself into a trance
Before he writing," and before he dance.
He always asking animals for views,
And now he make believe he dead Ted Hughes.

R.I.P. ROBERT WALLACE
January 10, 1932 – April 9, 1999

He did not flinch, he did not stint
To put his friends' verse into print.
Here lies in *Bits*, with slender solace,
The printer poet Robert Wallace.

R.I.P. RHINA ESPAILLAT
January 20, 1932 –

Wander among these monuments
And try to make of rime some sense;
You won't unless you ponder at
A stone marked "Rhina Espaillat."

R.I.P. JOHN UPDIKE
March 18, 1932 – January 27, 2009

His verse was often bright and funny
Unlike his prose which was not sunny
Except for *Eastwick* with its witches —
The movie kept the world in stitches.

R.I.P. HERBERT COURSEN
March 28, 1932 – December 3, 2011

Here lies the Bowdoin poet Herbert Coursen
Who never met a rime he couldn't force in.
He'd too much talent to be a poetaster,
So he became the small-time contest master.

R.I.P. SYLVIA PLATH
October 27, 1932 – February 11, 1963

Her father died, and then her spouse
Turned out to be an English louse,
She thought; therefore, she'd show her wrath
By turning off the beaten Plath.

R.I.P. LEWIS TURCO
May 2, 1934 –

Here lies at last and out of work,
The syllabubble wordsmith Turk
Who finds he cannot now resort
For rime to his sidekick Wesli Court.

R.I.P. LEROI JONES
October 7, 1934 –

Born LeRoi Jones, he hated white,
So took a Muslim name to spite
Every goddam Southun cracka
And wound up Amiri Baraka.

R.I.P. ROBERT MEZEY
February 28, 1935 –

Here lies a modern Aristotle
Whose pentametric power
Turned to and then against the Beat
Outside the Yvory tower.

R.I.P. MORTON MARCUS
September 6, 1936 – October 28, 2009

Here lies the offbeat Dreamer
Whose beard wound round his nose.
His rage, created by the world,
Was vented on a rose.

R.I.P. TED KOOSER
April 25, 1939 –

Ted Kooser
Was hardly a loser.
One of the aureate,
He became Laureate.

R.I.P. JACK FOLEY
August 9, 1940 –

Here lies Jack Foley
Decomposing slowly.
When he composed faster
It was a disaster.

R.I.P. DAVID WALKER
Oct. 13, 1942 – April 8, 2008

A son of Maine, where he was born,
That's where he died, his time outworn,
But much too soon, for Death's a stalker
Who overtook our David Walker.

R.I.P. SHARON OLDS
November 19, 1942 –

A poet, by birthright a Scorpio,
Kept trying to rime the word "Scorpio."
      She tried and she tried
      Till in torment she died
After dropping the *d* from *torpe[d]o*.*

R.I.P. JOSEPH S. SALEMI

February 1, 1948 –

The poet Joseph S. Salemi
Confronted readers with dilemmi:
How to read with solemn laughter
And forget his work thereafter.

R.I.P. CAROL FROST

February 28, 1948 –

Carol Frost would not be bossed,
Would not be limited or lost,
Yet here she lies and cannot sing:
The mud has stopped her Caroling.

R.I.P. R. S. GWYNN

May 13, 1948 –

Raised in the age of the atom bomb,
Sam never went to Vietnam,
And though he lived to use e-mail,
He never wore a ponytail.

He made us laugh, he made us giggle,
But now he makes the earthworms wiggle —
He smoked until they let him in:
Here lie the ashes of R. S. Gwynn.

R.I.P. BILL BAER

December 29, 1948 –

Erato taught him how to chime,
And he arrayed his lines with rime
Till he ran out of threads to wear —
Now time has worn our poor Bill Baer.

R.I.P. DANA GIOIA
December 24, 1950 –

He stopped upsetting apple carts
And led an Endowment for the Arts.
Now dead male poets can enjoy a
Fellowship with Dana Gioia.

R.I.P. ANNIE FINCH
October 31, 1956 –

Averse to logic, Annie Finch
In argument won't give an inch.
She'll spar and duck and even clinch —
But change her mind? You'd need a winch.

ENVOI: FOR THE UNKNOWN POETS

Here they lie, all the unknowns,
Reduced to ashes, dust and bones.
The songs they sang with lip and tongue
Have fallen still and lie among
The tattered leaves in a fold of time
Covered now with moss and rime.

EPILOGUE: THE MEWS OF POETRY
Or, Chasing Erato

R.I.P. BOZO

The first cat that we ever had
Was always good and never bad,
And so we petted him, of course,
Till he was stepped on by a horse.

R.I.P. REGGIE

A backward tiger, Regit
Betook himself to college,
Became a UConn husky
To gain a bit of knowledge.

We took him home with us
Where he used his education
To live a wise and happy life
Till he took this long vacation.

R.I.P. SCOOTER

If someone got into the tub
Scooter fished for toes
Till he fell in and stood forlorn
In water to his nose.

But he was born a wanderer
And often left to roam
The neighborhood and far beyond
Till he found another home.

R.I.P. POOKAH

The words upon his banner, if unfurled,
Would read, "The greatest cat in all the world
Lies here below puffing on his hookah.
Make your obeisance to majestic Pookah!"

R.I.P. CRAZY

Yes, he was well and truly named,
Our craziest by far.
Cross-eyed and manic till one day
He ran beneath a car.

R.I.P. SMOKY AND BIANCA

Bianca was a lady,
Plouffy as a pillow,
With one blue eye and one of green,
As graceful as a willow.

Smoky was her fellow,
Black to the nth degree,
As manly as a feline male
Could ever hope to be.

They could not be apart for long —
Where she went he would follow,
So they have gone where lovers go
And left behind a hollow.

R.I.P. SEEGER

Seeger was part Siamese
And black as any knave —
Although he looked piratical
He wasn't very brave.

If any enemy approached
To threaten our front door,
He'd jump upon our mailbox there
And emit his alto roar.

R. I. P. SWEETIE-PIE

Here lies pretty Sweetie-Pie,
Black of pelt, amber of eye,
Who loved to purr and take a nap
Upon an old man's welcome lap.
May her repose be dark and deep.
Let roses grow where she must sleep.

ABOUT THE AUTHOR

"Wesli Court" is the anagram pen-name that Lewis Turco, author of *The Book of Forms*, uses when he writes his traditionally formal poems and modern versions of Medieval verse.